Killing Jovenel

The Assassination of the President of Haiti

Written by:
Bobb Rousseau

The events I described are true

Fargo Style Disclaimer

"This is a true story. The events depicted in this podcast took place in Port-au-Prince, Haiti on 7 July 2021. To keep the story authentic, the names have not been changed. Out of respect for the dead, the story has been told exactly as it occurred.

Episode 1: The Sacrificial Lamb

{*Intro*}

Hello, and welcome to another true crime series, "Killing Jovenel," on Azazel Podcast. This series is about the savage assassination of the President of Haiti, Jovenel Moïse, on July 7, 2021. Here, I discussed the plausible causes leading up to the assassination of the President of Haiti and how such a gruesome assassination altered the outcomes of Haitian democracy and the country's diplomatic ties with other foreign nations.

I am your host Dr. Bobb Rousseau. Without further ado, let's begin.

[Outro]

Haitian political history is an open wound. The past never stays in the past. Every single event that happened once will happen again in the future. Haiti's political landscape has always been filled with corrupt presidents who let the oligarch run the country's economy as they receive orders from the international community. These influential presidents finish their terms with support from Haiti's wealthiest and foreign governments. However, presidents who fight against the corrupt oligarchy and demonstrate a solid will to reevaluate international aid are the exception leading the country without international support and do not finish their terms. They are either killed while in power or removed from power to be taken into exile by the international community. To the likes, I cite Jean-Jacques Dessalines, Toussaint Louverture, Dumarsais Estime, Jean-Bertrand Aristide, and Jovenel Moïse. Because their economic policies would have reduced the poverty gap and provided economic opportunities for the people to pursue the Haitian Dream, they infuriated Haiti's elite and their international backers. As a result, the country suffers as they are labeled as dictators, out of touch, gang enablers, and other similar degrading terms.

The book-podcast "Killing Jovenel" by Dr. Bobb Rousseau portrays Jovenel Moïse as the sacrificial lamb for the Let my Country Take Off Movement. There are many Haitian leaders, and there will be more to come with the energy to defend the poor and the middle class. When they become presidents, they will be assassinated or removed from power. "Killing Jovenel" shows that anyone with an economic policy and an education plan to improve Haitian agriculture and literacy is a Jovenel and, therefore, must be overthrown by all means possible because they rebel against the status quo.

The assassination of Jovenel started with that of Dessalines, and it sure does not end with Jovenel. So, it is because the roots of Haiti's fight for freedom tree will never stop rising. Each time that situation arises, there will be a president to lead the revolution. That president will be disempowered, ultimately killed, but another will rise until one branch grows powerfully popular to muster support from those who have been blocking its flourishment.

[Outro]

Killing Jovenel

On July 7, 2021, twenty-six Colombians entered the residence of the president of Haiti, Jovenel Moïse. They assassinated him savagely with no resistance from the General Security Unit of the National Palace, whose mission, among others, was to ensure the safety and security of the private residences of current and former presidents of the Republic. The police officers protecting the president and his family as the event unfolded did not fire a single shot.

Why do they kill him? Did he deserve to die? Did someone tell the police officers to stand down no matter what? What is next for the country's rule of law?

Stay tuned to learn more about the despicable assassination of the President of Haiti, The Honorable His Excellency, Mr. Jovenel Moïse.

Episode 2: Jovenel Moise

{Intro}

Hello, and welcome back to Azazel Podcast. In this series, we will be exploring all about JOVENEL MOÏSE. Who he was, and subsequently, the circumstances surrounding his assassination. Every notable assassination in the past has a common background—they were all leaders. Abraham Lincoln of the United States, Mahatma Gandhi of India, and Malcolm X of the United States—all these figures were leaders who were killed by an act of political violence.

Join us as we dive deep into the assassination of Haitian president JOVENEL MOÏSE. Let's delve into this juicy information without further ado, shall we?

{Segue}

While Jovenel Moise was a leader, we cannot forget that he was first a citizen interested in politics before his election in 2016.

On June 26, 1968, the middle child family of Etienne Moïse and Lucia Bruno, a merchant, and a seamstress, gave birth to Jovenel Moïse in Trou-du-Nord, Haiti's North-East department. Not long after his arrival, the family moved from Trou-du-Nord to Port-au-Prince in 1974. From the neighborhood of Port-au-Prince, Jovenel did both his primary and secondary school education before walking the part to Universté Quisqueya, where he studied Political science. Interestingly, he met his life partner during his university journey. Romantic, isn't that?

From his childhood experience, Jovenel had developed the mindset for development - that he did by leaving the capital in 1996 with his wife - Martine Joseph and moving to Port-de-Paix to fulfill the goal of developing rural areas through agriculture. In Port-de-Paix, he launched his first mechanic business, JOMAR Auto Parts, with little capital investment; surprisingly, JOMAR still exists.

And that same year, he had his agribusiness rolling. He built his first Agriculture Project. There, he set up a banana plantation in the Northwest department, which was his focus till 2016, when he became President of Haiti.

Not long after he started his Agribusiness, as the lover of development that he was, he saw the need for access to clean water by the people of the hinterland and yet embarked on a new project of giving them access to clean water. He achieved that in partnership with the company Culligan of Port-au-Prince and loans from financial institutions. At last, he solved the problem and started a water plant to distribute clean drinking water to the people of the Northeast and Northwest of Haiti.

He started his journey into the political world to further furnish his interest in community development. He joined the Chamber of Commerce and the Northwest Industry (CCINO). From there, his political tales knew no bounds. From being the Secretary General of the Chamber of Commerce and Industry in Haiti (CHIC) to becoming the founder of the Haitian Energy

Company SA (COMPHENER SA), a company aimed at bringing solar and wind energy to ten communes of the Northwest department. After that, he entered the national political stage to become President.

Even with the chain of political controversies in Haiti, Jovenel had always built an interest in politics, which he entered through the business world. While the political situation has never been in his favor, especially with the annulment of the 2015 election, where he won and later emerged as the winner the second time in the 2016 Election, he was sworn in as the Haiti President in February 2017, following an extended and complicated two-year election cycle. His swearing-in led to his sweet and sour administration and life.

Almost everyone who knew Jovenel knew him through his presidency, and I must explain that part of him because it shows the higher part of who he was and as whom he will be remembered.

Thus, while he had it all great to be in that leadership position, the nation of Haiti never had it easy, especially with the ongoing violence engulfing the streets. That showed in the mass demonstrations two years into his administration. Two years later, he started ruling by decree, and the democratic future of Haiti was erased. The protest happened in September 2019 and was reported to have killed at least seventeen people and injured almost two hundred around the country. Not only that, many businesses, government officials, and buildings bore the brunt of the citizens' wrath.

Should I say his ruling by decree and being an apprentice dictatorial leader was who he was and that his leadership had led to mass demonstrations and unrest? Well, a bit of it reflected who he was, and since his administration has only witnessed rising inflation and low economic turnout, the demonstration is bound to happen one day. But then, his being an apprentice dictatorial leader reflected how much he wanted to save Haiti from the opposition leader. If you could not join them, you had to go harder than them - simply like Jovenel did. He declared, to show his clout right after becoming the only elected official in the country, and I quote: "After God, only I have the power to do whatever in the country." That was to boast that he was the only leader in command of the country.

Honestly, with a non-quorum Supreme Court and without the deputies, senators, municipal councils, and administration councils, he centralized all the republic's powers into his hands. Shortly after this declaration, the Haitian political world ignited and criticized him for wanting to be a dictator. Note that throughout his presidency, his various speeches and actions had earned him several trivial nicknames such as "Banana Man," "Little David," "After God," "The Promise Guy," "The 24/7 Electricity Man" and "Engineer" to name a few. The latter came after the Court of Auditors released the PetroCaribe fund report showing him signing his name with such an unearned title.

While I'll say he is an apprentice dictator but also indifferent and strong-willed. Irrespective of what the opposition was pushing him to leave power, he did not budge. Haiti's politics has always been complicated, favoring only the survival of the strongest. These reflect the ongoing struggles and chaos in Haiti.

However, this makes me question, "how can Haiti suffer so much financial loss under a president who was himself a business mogul." Jovenel was an entrepreneur with many "sustainable development" businesses, including solar panels, a water plant, and a 10-hectare (25-acre) banana plantation in the Nord-Ouest. His vast business knowledge earned him a reputation in Haiti's agribusiness and political circles.

For someone who had promised bio-ecological agriculture as an engine for Haitian economic recovery and had a vision of using agriculture to create jobs and generate wealth for the populace, 50% of it was the rural people. I have a question: Where did all the savvy business knowledge go? Did he lose when he entered politics and became President? Or did he lose them when he began enjoying the power that compelled him to act, as many claimed, as a dictator? Was that all a facade to get the people's vote?

But then, revealing who Jovenel is has furnished more interest in knowing the person behind his assassination. Could it be the opposition party who wants him gone, as his tenure was believed to have reached its term? Could it be a known or an unknown enemy? Did the multiple protests meshed with his stance against the oligarchy give other people the opportunity to take advantage of the situation?

We will get into that in the next episode. Have a beautiful week!

Episode 3: Assassins

{Intro}

His ruling, as the people called him, "an apprentice dictator whose dream was to leave poverty and be a part of development, ended with his assassination on July 7, 2021.

Hello, welcome back to another episode of Azazel Podcast. In today's episode, I explain more about JOVENEL MOÏSE's death. I'll be answering that question - Who Killed Him?

In the last episode, I talked about who he was, but today I will let you know more about the person behind his assassination. Here on this Azazel Podcast today, we will see whether it was someone from the opposition party or perhaps an unknown enemy, and I will unravel all that in this episode.

{Segue}

The question of who killed Jovenel comes with much rhetoric, but then from popular information, he was assassinated and shot dead in his home on July 7, 2021. While we all knew through the last episode that his tenure as the president came with many controversies, especially having thousands of citizens protest for his resignation and the demand for the prosecution of those who looted $2 billion from the government's Petrocaribe Fund.

With that, was also the fact that kidnapping grew to become a criminal enterprise, which decreased the people's purchasing power as he failed to organize elections to renew the parliament's upper and lower chambers. All these happenings were surrounding his presidential tenure and just before his assassination. Can I say his assassination is what the citizens ever wanted to end the governance?

This motive behind his assassination will further help discover who must have killed him. Don't you agree with me on that? While the country seems to have a problem with his administration, many citizens are still dumbfounded by the fact that he can be killed. Let's start by making an elimination process to find the culprit.

Ever since the protest in 2019, there has been an increase in armed gangs that seems to have unclear allegiance but has not ceased from terrorizing the country. They have continued to control the growing portion of the country by kidnapping and gang-raping citizens. Can it be said that these armed gangs are the killer? Absolutely No?

One of the videos reported to have been shot at the assassination scene is that whoever killed him is related to people in the U.S. Drug Enforcement Administration. However, this gruesome murder was carried out not only by well-trained professional killers but commandos since only well-trained assassins can overpower the presidency's security.

Another news was communicated by Haiti's State secretary for communications - Frantz Exantus, on Twitter, where he announced that some of the suspects in the assassination had been captured. On the other hand, the police mentioned a group of mercenaries, most of whom were Colombians to be the assailants - to be exact, 26 of them were Colombians, and there were two Haitian Americans. The police further supported that claim with a Haitian doctor, Mr. Sanon Emmanuel, who they believed was a suspect and one behind the attack. He was thought to have ordered these people to become president.

Additionally, an investigating judge was appointed to look into this. In the investigation that was conducted further, the two suspected Haitian Americans stated that they had no prior knowledge of the assassination. They had only been hired as an interpreter for the Columbians since Haiti's official languages were Creole and French, while that of the Columbians is Spanish, and they happen to speak both.

On the other hand, the Colombians stated that they had only been hired to provide security. Many Colombians are retired armed officers and, after retirement, go to security firms where they're hired for their expertise. That seemed like what they had been employed for rather than assassination.

But who must be this someone - who must have hired these people as security, but who can this be? That brings me to another critical suspect - Haitian 63-year-old doctor Christian Emmanuel Sanon. Haitian police chief - Leon Charles stated that Mr. Sanon hired the 28 Columbians through a Miami-based company called CTU, run by Venezuelan national Tony Intriago. Aside from that fact that gives Sanon away as a suspect, he was the first person the Colombian suspects called when the police surrounded them. Isn't that suspicious?

The police chief later clarified that it seems the Columbians have been duped of the role they were earlier appointed for - which was to protect Emmanuel Sanon. But one way or the other, that mission changed.

Former Haitian senator John Joel Joseph, another suspect in the case, was arrested as he was believed to oversee ammunition supplies and meeting arrangements. With his arrest is another suspect taken to be on the run - Mr. Joseph Felix Badio, a former official in the justice ministry's anti-corruption unit. All the suspects do have a connection with the Haiti political circuit. The question of "who the killer was" has become more attractive.

Whereas this remains speculation, everything regarding the assassination is still unclear. Many people believed to have a connection with the assassination were arrested, and a dozen others are still on the loose. Even with all this speedy progress in the earlier days of the assassination, the investigation has been slow for the past months. Details about the assailants are still vague, and the motives behind the assassination remain unclear.

Nothing less than five successive judges have overseen the case, but none of these judges have issued any charges for the forty people currently imprisoned in connection with it. It seems more of the judging power has been left to the U.S. Is this related to the constitution that is not working? All these will be explained more in subsequent episodes.

{Outro}

Killing Jovenel

Over a year since his assassination, it seems like Jovenel is fast being forgotten. The president's assailant has not been found, and the mystery continues to linger in many of the citizens' hearts and how much they are protected from the assassination's aftermath. Whoever killed him must have imagined this and be the one whose assassination of Jovenel will benefit. The investigation is stalling, and the whole system itself is crumbling. Haiti's search for the assailant continues.

And so, the search continues - Who killed Jovenel Moïse?

See you again! Don't forget to hit the subscribe button.

Episode 4: Savages

{Intro}

Hello, welcome back to another episode of Azazel Podcast. In today's episode, I'll explain more about JOVENEL MOÏSE's death.

In the last episode, I talked about who killed him, but today I will let you know more about how he was killed. While it might sound gory, his death must be talked about. Here on this Azazel Podcast today, I will talk about the whole movement in the way he was killed and how that happened.

{Segue}

Almost everyone prays to die in their sleep, but because life happens, some die through assassination or other gruesome ways. One of them is Jovenel. Jovenel, a 53-years old Haiti President who had lived amidst poverty to build himself up through his Agribusiness and work his way up to the political space of Haiti - The presidency. But his almost five-year presidency ended with his death. The President of Haiti had his last moment feeling unprotected. Just like every other citizen of Haiti that has died through assassination and at the hands of gunmen, the President himself is not left out.

Jovenel was gruesomely murdered by some hired assassins in his home on July 7, 2021. His private home outside Port-au-Prince was attacked brazenly at 01:00 local time, according to police. The first shot was heard in the neighborhood precisely at 1:00

am local time. The gun shattered the sweet dreams of not only the President himself and his family but also everyone in the community. It was unbelievable that an attack was ongoing in the President's villa. Someone believed to be in the best position to have the best protection.

According to one of the investigating judges, the President was shot twelve times in the head by the assailants leading to several bullet wounds in his head and torso. His left eye was gouged out, and bones in his arm and his knees and ankles were broken. Jovenel died at the scene and was found lying on the floor on his back, in blood. The pain would have been unbearable if he were to be saved.

That brazen attack had his wife, First Lady - Martine shot and wounded. Still, gracefully, she escaped death and was hospitalized at the South Florida Hospital right after the assassination. The First Lady stated in her interview with the New York Times that they were asleep when woken by gunshots. She called for help from the security team, and none was forthcoming. She could only see the assailants in their bedroom, shooting her husband and herself.

They left thinking she was dead.

On the morning of the assassination, bullet casings were found outside the President's private apartment, showing that multiple shots had been fired that early into the night. When the video footage taken by residents was checked, men were covered in black and all arriving in different vehicles.

In the video, a man thought to be the security guard was made to lie flat on the street, and his weapons were seized. With him being disarmed, the video shows another man who most likely was one of the assailants and happened to be shouting into the loudspeaker in English, "DEA [US Drug Enforcement Administration} operation, everybody stays down!"

One of the President's neighbors - Ralph Chevry, who happens to be a civil servant, explained how he had never heard of the gunshot before in Haiti. This makes it more plausible when the assailants were presumed to be Columbians. Other neighbors confirmed how they listened to the assailants speaking in Spanish.

But what was surprising was they used the US DEA as a cover-up as there was no way the DEA would be shouting to show their presence and disarmed a security officer. The whole killing seems even more suspicious because with many bullets lying around, only the President and his wife were shot. Were they the only target of this assassination, or is there more to see than what everyone is being fed?

Indeed, there might be more.

What's more, the presidential guards, who were close to 50, were nowhere to be found at the scene of the incident, and none had been reported to be injured; while that was good news, it is hard to understand why they did not show up to protect the country. Presidential Security should have been found to protect him from the assailants. Before the attack in July, Jovenel had earlier stated in January in a report by the Washington Post that he was a subject of an assassination attempt and a planned coup.

But all that was only counted by the opposition party to reinforce that the Jovenel administration is filled with kidnapping and gang violence. Only if he had known the assassination attempt would prepare him for the worst yet to come - His death. Even a day before the attack, he had announced his new prime minister, Dr. Ariel Henry. Further showing that he didn't see, feel, or know the evil that would befall him the next day.

Of the new suspected assailants, three suspects had died, and 18 others had not been charged yet. What is next after the death of President Jovenel? Will everything eventually get back to normal, or will the chaos continue? The need to uncover the truth behind his death is paramount since it will help build a better Haiti with an excellent future for its citizens. Does his assassination signify a denial of the government's accountability?

If the President were not safe in his own home, then no one in Haiti would be safe; hopefully, justice will be served soon, and the country will rest. Even I think Jovenel would have wanted to see peace in Haiti after his death.

Stay subscribed to be among the first to listen to our next story on JOVENEL coming on the podcast.

Episode 5: House rats eat House Straw

{Intro}

Welcome to another episode of Killing Jovenel on Podcast Azazel. In today's episode, I'll explain more about JOVENEL MOÏSE's death and expose some of the suspects that were found to have killed him.

Who do you think they are?

In the last episode, I talked about how he was killed in his home in the wee hours of July 07, 2021, at his home in Pèlerin 5 in Haiti's Capital. Today, I'll talk more about the suspects involved in his case, who they are, and what must have made them kill him or get involved in his death. You are ready to get on that ride with me, aren't you?

{Segue}

When a president is assassinated, a rigorous investigation follows into who the killers might have been. Jovenel was also not an exception; I believe the process was just a little different. Catching even the suspects was a bit slow as those who carried out the act were still unknown three days after the 26 Colombians and allies assassinated the President.

But about a few weeks later, over 26 suspects were arrested for the assassination. The suspects include Haiti-Americans, Colombian mercenaries, some policemen, and high-ranking officials in Haiti. This isn't surprising as Jovenel was never the people's man, nor was he the Oligarchs' sweetheart, and I can call him a one-person army.

You will remember that in the last episode, the assailants assassinated him without any intrusion from the President's security guards. That is quite alarming considering the heavy security personnel a President must have. From the happenings, one would either think the President's security guards worked in tandem with the assailants or might have even been the ones who made those foreigners take the bait. However, whoever it is, we will find it all out.

In episode two, I made mention of the Colombians who were taken in as suspects. However, upon interrogation, they only told the police that they were security officials and had only been to Haiti because they thought they were appointed to arrest the President; upon getting there they only found he was dead. This is the same with other personnel arrested as suspects, who all denied having a connection with his death. But who can we believe when the surviving wife heard the assailants conversing over the phone about a file?

No one was left out of the search for the assailants. Even four police officers and a judge were arrested as suspects. Jean Laguel Civil, who served as general security coordinator on the night of the President's assassination, was arrested. Even the Superior Court Judge Windelle Coq-Thélot was not left out of this. Dimitri Herard, the President's Palace Security Chief, was also held in for questioning. Dimitri Herard was believed to have traveled in many countries to allegedly meet with high ranking individuals to plan the assassination while Jean Laguel Civil was the one with large sums of money to distribute to the guards who were present at the killing scene. Surprisingly, two new suspects were found by the Haiti police and were found to possess a lot of weapons. That makes it more plausible that they might have been involved in the assassination. These two suspects were identified as Reynaldo Covington and Gilbert Dragon.

The research discovered Joseph Felix Badio had conversations with Reynaldo Covington, Jude Gilbert Dragon, and others between January and July 2021. Gilbert Dragon was responsible for providing precise information on the acts and gestures of Jovenel to Joseph Felix Badio. Not only was he found to be responsible for this, but he was also responsible for being an informant for the Commando with Drug Enforcement Administration (DEA) logo for the assassination operation between July 6 to July 7, 2021, in the capital city of Haiti, Port-au-Prince.

He was arrested about a month after the assassination on August 1, 2021, and charged with the case at hand, the President's assassination. But unfortunately for him and even the investigating team, Marie Jude Gilbert DRAGON died on November 17, 2021, at the Civil Prison located at Port-au-Prince under unclear circumstances.

While the cause of his death seems unclear, it was reported that he died from acute respiratory distress. When he was found out to have had this, several requests were made to the judicial authorities to authorize his transfer to a hospital center outside the prison; even one was made two days before his death. When the request was granted two days after and he was authorized to leave the jail for a hospital, he died the same day at the hospital.

After his death, the same goes for the other suspects, who were detained and nothing else, not even trial or arraignment. To get to the bottom of who killed him, why he was killed, and all involved, every sector should not be left out, the communication sector, the transportation, and even the banking sectors. All of these have been used to aid their involvement in the assassination. If further investigations are done in this regard, it will not only give hope to the people of Haiti to believe in Human Rights but will also put even the minds of Jovenel Moise at rest because they know their father's assailants.

{Outro}

The search is still not ending here; it continues. Who is behind the death of Jovenel must be uncovered, and not just speculations on who are assailants? Even after a year, some of these suspects haven't been prosecuted but are still awaiting trials.

Thank you for listening to today's episode. I hope you enjoyed it just as much as I loved recording it. Stay subscribed to be among the first to listen to our next story on JOVENEL coming on the podcast.

Episode 6: Intelligence and Security Detail

{*Intro*}

Hello and welcome back to another episode of Killing Jovenel on Azazel Podcast. In the last episode, I showed that, according to official reports from renowned newspapers and the Haitian judicial system, it was the house rats that ate the house straw, meaning that the head of the president was deeply involved in the president's massacre. In this episode, I poke holes that exposed the weakness of the president's protection and the security of his private residence.

On July 7, 2021, at 1:00 am, twenty-six Colombians invaded the premises of the private residence of the president of Haiti, His Excellence, Honorable Jovenel Moïse. One group entered the house, passed down the hall, walked through a room decorated with Haitian handicrafts, and continued to the main bedroom, where they opened fire and executed the president. After that, they looted and opened drawers, closets, and cupboards to look for documents, jewelry, and money. The other group stayed in the house to watch the Haitian guards; all that happened without the intervention of any presidential security guard. By 1:30 am, the assassins were gone. Did you see how easy it was for the Colombians to commit the most gruesome crimes in political history?

The USGPN was supposed to be the secret service responsible for providing presidential protection, yet they did not protect the president on the day of the assassination. The freshly empowered National Intelligence Agency (ANI) was supposed to apply meticulous advance work and threat assessments to identify and deter potential risks to the country. Yet, the Colombians assassinated Jovenel Moise right under their nose. That compelled us to analyze the security layout of the president's private residence to determine whether his security details and the country's intelligence agency had the means to use advanced countermeasures to deter, minimize and decisively respond to identified threats and vulnerabilities.

Jovenel lived in a rental property in Pèlerin 5, less than a mile from the heavily guarded Taiwan Embassy. The presidential residence was a simple one-story house with a single entry and exit for vehicles and pedestrians. Jovenel was supposed to be protected by a security detail of about ten police officers from the USGPN. I bet you a pickle that these officers were dozing off or playing with their phones throughout the assassination. The road that led to the president's private residence had no security checkpoints and was open to anyone.

Many are wondering whether it was a good idea for a president to live in a rented house without ANI's approval and without them conducting thorough assessments, surveillance, reconnaissance, and analyzes to identify possible threats to national security. There I wonder whether they at least checked the landlord's credentials or whether the president told anyone he was renting such a property. As president, Jovenel was as unprotected as the guy who sleeps outside in a cardboard box. Granted that the police questioned the landlord, but such a background check was supposed to be completed before the president signed the rental agreement.

If the guards wanted to intervene to stop the assassination, did they have the required training to do? At the time, Jovenel was the most hated man in the world, and it seemed that the guards did not care about him too much and were ready, if asked, to betray him. That showed that these police officers did not get to be part of the president's security detail based on their qualifications but their political connection with high-ranking officials.

I think these guards' abilities, or their lack thereof, to assure the president's safety was no match to that of the Colombians. These hired Colombians were ex-military personnel with commendable experience in ground combat and providing high-level security to various levels of powerful families worldwide. However, that should not have prevented the Haitian guards from accessing the Colombians to Haiti'sHaiti's first powerful family.

{*Ouro*}

I will hold on blaming them too much because, even if they could fight back, their back was against the wall. After all, early reports detailed that they received money from Dimitri Hérard, Moïse's chief of security, and Jean-Laguel Civil, Jovenel Moïse's security head. Other police officers, such as Boni Gregoire, Clifton Hyppolite, and Elie Jean Charles, were arrested, while at least 35 were fired in connection with the president's murder fallout.

Thanks for listening and remember to come back soon for another suspenseful episode of Killing Jovenel.

Episode 7: Why the Killing

{Intro}

Hello, welcome back to another episode of {Azazel Podcast. In today's episode, I will explain more about JOVENEL MOÏSE's death. I will be answering that question - Why was he killed?

In the last episode, I talked about how he was killed, how scary it was for his wife, and how alarming it was to find that none of his Presidential security was wounded. The way he was killed left suspicion flying around. This suspicion led to this episode of knowing why he was murdered. Why will a president be assassinated? What had he done to deserve to be killed in his home?

All that will be explained on the podcast today. Stay tuned to this episode, and let's get digging!

{Segue}

Since the death of Jovenel Moïse, the late president of Haiti had been announced, the country has been thrown further into a state of turmoil. The danger keeps looming on every citizen, and many have left the country to further avert themselves from the impending dangers lurking around the country.

With Haiti thrown into a state of confusion, so also is the investigation of the president's death. The investigation has been slow, and only a few hints have been dropped on why he was killed. Jovenel Moïse had been a president who found his way to the political stage after his days as a businessman.

In his early days, he has always been interested in the development and Agriculture business, which he did by working on water implants in the rural part of Haiti and on his banana farm. Decades after he became known in Agribusiness, he found his way into politics. He took the Haiti mantle of leadership by becoming the president after his election in 2016, where he emerged the winner. He was sworn in in 2017, and not quite long after he started his presidency, Haiti lost its democracy, becoming a victim of Jovenel's rule by decree.

Jovenel entered the presidential administration as a civilian but ended it as an authoritarian ruler. Unfortunately, Jovenel was murdered in the comfort of his home on July 7, 2021, and that attack had his wife injured, but none of his security men were wounded.

Every citizen wondered why he was killed, and even his wife stated in her interview with New York Times that it must have been the oligarchs and the system of Haiti that had the president killed. How true is that? What must have been the reason to kill him? or even at that, what had the first lady seen to proclaim that?

Martine - Jovenel's wife, who was a victim of attempted murder and had witnessed her husband's gruesome death, saw the assailants take something where her husband always kept his files and heard the assailants speak in Spanish, showing that they were not Haitian citizens. To further illustrate how much suspicion the attack carries, the wife listened to the assailants conversing with someone on the phone while they carried out their operation.

Was that the operation's lead, or had the person sent them to get the files? What was in that file, and is the file the reason they killed the president? I know how so much of that is arising in my mind and the mind of every listener of this podcast. But I tell you, we will get to the root of the problem.

After a series of investigations, 20 Columbians were arrested for the murder, and 2 Haitian Americans were arrested. Surrounding these arrests is the claim on the political mantle from which the president's death came. The probability that the reason the president was killed is related to political space is high. Emmanuel Sanon, who was earlier detained for the murder, had shown interest in the country's presidency. He was stated to have arrived at Haiti's airport in a private airplane with a sole objective - to be politically involved.

To understand his death, Haitian police have conducted international hunting, and many people have been sentenced and arrested in either the US, Turkey, or Miami. They have been arraigned based on extradition laws. The Turkish authorities detained a man considered a suspect of great interest in the president's assassination. This suspect, named Samira Handal, was believed to have been part of the plot. Although, he denied the charges and stood on the ground that he only rented out places for the suspects caught in the assassination. He claimed not to have any mutual relationship with the doctor who was indicted as a suspect rather than a client-based relationship since he only rented an office to the doctor in question. The Turkish government later released Handal.

Emmanuel Sanon, the doctor in question, was one of the suspects arrested for the president's assassination because the Columbians called him after their arrest. The plot to kidnap the president only resulted in his death and further a state of confusion for the country.

The Haiti police have continued to hunt for suspects everywhere, but none of the suspects could give a motive for their murder. There has been no reason for the death, and only people whose identity remains a mystery to the police are those they have in custody. How hard it is to become a president and how hard it is to die unjustly.

{Outro}

The more complex the search, the deeper what was found raises more questioning. Why the president was killed remains a mystery, the author and mastermind behind his assassination are still behind the scenes. But then, the search continues as always!!

Follow and subscribe to the podcast for more updates on the death of Jovenel Moïse and what begets the nation of Haiti, and how much is needed to be done to recover from the loss.

Episode 8: International Meddling

{Intro}

ello, welcome back to another episode of Azazel Podcast. In today's episode, I'll discuss JOVENEL MOÏSE's death. Together, we will see what the international community has been doing to help. Why are they involved, or should they have kept to them since it is a Haiti matter?

In the last episode, I talked about what has been done so far to catch his killers. How much they have found and the farther the years go by, the nearer we're to the reality that the Haiti police officials always stall investigation progress and draw citizens and families of concerned victims to the continuation of the investigation.

In previous episodes, we have seen help from the international community, and we will be discussing it extensively in this episode. What is Haiti's relationship with the United States, and how are all these people involved in the assassination of a president?

It is becoming more interesting.

{Segue}

The death of [a] nobody concerns no one; however, the end of a well-known person becomes the talk of the town. This phrase only speaks more of the Haiti President, Jovenel Moïse, who was assassinated at his private residence in the capital, Port-au-Prince, on July 7, 2021. The President was murdered coldly, and the murderer had his wife severely injured, but his children were safe.

With his death comes the colossal truth - indeed, something must be buried even if the President must be the sacrifice for it. And what could that thing be? It is still yet unknown since the killer has not been found.

Haiti, a Caribbean country that remains one of the poorest countries in the Latin American and Caribbean (LAC) region and even in the world, has had its share of poverty, bad governance, and natural disasters. Finding her way through the allocation of cholera in 2014 and hurricane in 2016, and with a ray of hope for a better future elected Jovenel as President and swore him in in 2017. But as history would have it, all dreams were shattered with Jovenel's autocratic rule and, finally, his assassination in 2021, which only spiked more violence in the country.

With these natural disasters and human rights violation history comes the intervention from international communities. After a state of emergency was declared by the prime minister of Haiti against the death of the President and it was found out that the suspects were not Haiti citizens, the call from international communities was inevitable.

On Friday, July 9, 2021, the United States was the first to show its involvement, which it did through the United States Law enforcement and Intelligence Agency. They ensured that the Haiti-American citizens found to be suspects were investigated.

In tandem with this is the revelation by two members of the United States government sources who identified a former informant of the Drug Enforcement Administration as an accomplice in the assassination of the President. The suspect, Joseph Vincent, a 55-year-old man who lived in Florida, was believed to have taken part in the attack that took the President's life alongside James Solages.

The two men told the Haiti Investigators they had been hired to serve as interpreters on a team dominated by 26 Colombians. Even if the killer was not caught yet, the international community did show some level of commitment that has thus helped the Haiti Police force this far.

To some extent, it looks more like the international communities are making efforts toward catching the killer than the Haiti National police. But I believe it is not enough because the suspects are essentially not Haiti citizens.

With a level of suspicion in the President's assassination, another shocking news was bound to be heard. In an interview with New York Times, Ryan Grim, the arrested Drug Enforcement Agency Informant who was arrested as a suspect in the assassination, stated that he had only been involved in the whole assassination process because he thought it had the United States support and backing. Shocking, isn't it? How can the United States be a party to the killing of a president when it had been at the forefront of assisting the country in finding the assailants?

Even though this seems almost like a piece of shocking news, the realization was bound to happen. Two months after the

President's death, the investigator in charge of the President's assassination discovered that there had been numerous communications through a phone call between the newly appointed Prime minister - Ariel Henry, and Joseph Felix, a former official with the Haiti government who was suspected of having overseen the operation.

Not only did Henry respond to this accusation from the investigator hastily, but he also even fired both Joseph and his boss. His hasty decision made him a suspect and even increased the support of the United States for him. The United States even issued another public statement to support Prime Minister Ariel Henry as the country's interim leader. I believe his identification as a suspect should strip him of his current position or, better still, prevent him from the position of ruling the country. But the reverse is the case.

To top it all, the Haiti-Americans arrested all have a connection with the United States, and even the suspected Colombians were working with a security firm in the United States and were previously trained by the United States.

Interestingly, Mr. Rivera, one of the suspected Columbians, had had previous assassination history, but that with Bolivia. He was believed to have entered Bolivia just before its presidential election as part of a plot to assassinate the presidential candidate. The outgoing right-wing defense minister masterminded this. This information raises more shocking news for Rivera; did he have the United States support to kill the Bolivian President?

While the story of whether the United States supported the assassination is still open to investigation, Haiti must stand on its own and protect its territory from too many external interventions.

{Outro}

The involvement of the international communities in Haiti's politics will only put the country into further problems than it currently is. If additional measures are not taken, it will take a while to bring Haiti back to a state of peace, especially with external interventions from the international community.

I look forward to reading all your opinions and comments, and don't forget to listen to the previous episodes to stay updated on the podcast.

See you all.

Episode 9: Catching the assassins

{Intro}

Hello, welcome back to another episode of Azazel Podcast. In today's episode, I'll explain more about JOVENEL MOÏSE's death. We will be delving together into what has been done so far. How has the investigation been, and what is the current mode on those who killed the President?

In the last episode, I talked about why he was killed; with the assailants taking an unknown document from the President's bookshelves and communicating with someone on the phone while they carried out their duties, the assassination had a mastermind to it. Albeit all these is the need to know what has been done so far to catch his killers. He is a president, and the best investigator must have been assigned to the Job.

Shall we get into that in this episode?

{Segue}

It will be callous to say it is not necessary for the killers to be found, aside from the fact that the President was the one being assassinated; finding the assailants will put the minds of Haitians at rest. The country will feel a deep peace that has been dead for a while now. While it is still unclear who might have murdered the President coldly and have his wife wounded, the Haiti Police and other international police hands have been on deck.

His death which happened on July 07, 2020, at his private residence in the capital of Haiti, Port-au-Prince, in the odd hours of the morning, had him being shot to death 12 times with each bullet piercing his body. His wife was also shot, but luckily, she made it to the hospital, where she was treated as an emergency patient.

The assassination caused a public uproar in the city of Haiti, and security officials were torn on how much could happen to the President overnight. The citizens are surprised at how the President could have been killed in his own home, giving them the obvious truth that no one in the country is safe. Even the international community is not left out in this way of killing and showing their support to the Haiti police in uncovering the truth about the murder.

What has been done so far can only be measured as successful if the killer had been found, but still, all the efforts for the past year cannot be disregarded. The acting prime minister, Claude Joseph, and police chief, Léon Charles, did declare a state of emergency in the country immediately after the President was buried as a first step to catching the killer.

First, a former police officer who was part of the Presidential security team was handed over to the Haiti police force as a suspect. The former police officer - Tanis Philome, was arrested in the Dominican Republic, even though he denied his involvement in the assassination.

Fortunately, they could get hold of some suspects who were believed to be the masterminds even though the arrest yielded no results regarding the motive for the assassination.

From the investigation so far, twenty Columbians and two Haitian Americans were arrested. These suspects claimed to have been recruited by a Florida-based doctor who hoped to replace Moise as the President, but the mission failed, and he is part of the suspect's list. That dream was aborted. While the arrest had four of the suspects shot in the process, the eighteen others still await trials.

Bits of help have been sought from the international communities; the Haiti police asked the White House for help identifying the killers as the assailants were assumed to have the DEA as a cover-up for their activities.

At the beginning of the incident, the police were seen almost everywhere to uncover the truth. But what changed? What stopped the police and investigating judges in their steps to uncover the truth? Truth be told, these officials must be tired, especially with the rate of kidnapping and gang-raping in Haiti now.

But still, it doesn't justify the fact that the investigation has been slow and the result it is yielding is low and not credible enough. In the end, it only shows that dozens have been arrested, few have been arraigned, and only small light has been shown on who the killer is. Indeed, more needs to be done to catch his killers, or perhaps the mantra from investigating officials -

L'enquête se poursuit — the investigation continues will be the end of the President's assassination.

{Outro}

What happens after your death is unknown to you, but the truth remains that what led to the end of Jovenel Moise should stop being a mystery, and the killer should be caught sooner than later.

See you all at the next episode and remember to get updates on the past episodes. Don't forget to subscribe and turn the alarm button.

Episode 10: Aftermath

{Intro}

Haiti witnessed cholera and is still trying to spring back, but with Jovenel's assassination, it seems like the dark end of the tunnel. His assassination abruptly ended a four-and-a-half-year presidency, bringing them even more problems than they had imagined.

In the last episodes, I explained more about the involvement of the international community in the political affairs of the country of Haiti and even in the President's assassination. It was found that the United States did back the assassination and, at the same time, helped get some suspects. Either way, all of these must have a toll on the whole of Haiti. In this episode, I will give you more insights into how Haiti has been after the assassination and what the country faced because of Jovenel Moise's assassination.

{Segue}

History has written yet another story for Haiti like it always has. Assassination has not always been a new thing in Haiti, even some past presidents have been assassinated before, and even some journalists were assassinated when Jovenel was the President. Just like every assassination, Haiti has witnessed, the President's own does not seem like an exception, the investigation appears to have hit a rocking button, and it is affecting even the country.

Weeks after the assassination, there was little clarity on who had the constitutional power to lead the country since the President was dead. Even though against the 1987 constitution that provides for the head of the supreme court to take over the presidency seat if vacant, Claude Joseph, who was the then acting Prime Minister, proclaimed himself as the interim President. However, since the death of the head of the Supreme Court due to COVID-19, it remains who is to fill the vacant seats.

To aggravate the matter, Jovenel had appointed a new prime minister before his assassination, Ariel Henry. Henry, a neurosurgeon, coordinated Haiti's response to the cholera pandemic in 2010 and served as the Minister of Interior during President Martelly's tenure in 2015. Henry swore in and ordered Joseph Claude to step down as the interim President and take the position of Foreign Minister. In the wake of this political instability is the rise of gang violence and insecurity with street violence in the country. The gangs seem to be using the weight of the political instability to grow in strength and influence.

In recent months, there has been an increase in the ways the rival gangs in Haiti operate, which has left many Haitians to become victims of deaths from gang violence and stray bullets. Many citizens living in the Croix-des-Bouquets part of Haiti have had numerous encounters with bullets pairing through the roofs of their houses. No one is safe in Haiti currently; many wake up to shells on the floor of their homes, while others do not wake up from sleep after being hit by stray bullets.

Around late April and early May of 2022, hundreds of lives were lost to the fight between the rival gangs – 400 Mawozo and Chen Mechan. All these happened in Croix-des-Bouquets and the capital of Haiti, Northeast of Port-au-Prince. The battle witnessed the destruction of many houses, and many people were burnt alive. Indeed, Haitians have been through a lot, and this is quite devastating.

Unfortunately, these attacks led to the displacement of about sixteen thousand women and girls in the country, as recorded by the National Human Rights Defense of Haiti. Many of the women and young girls were victims of repeated gang-raping by the gang members.

After the assassination, the country witnessed a change in power, the prime minister's ascension as Haiti's Interim leader was supported by the United States and the Core Group, which is an alliance that includes Canada, France, the United States, and representatives from the American States and the United Nations. Ariel Henry, the new Haiti Interim Leader, only exalted a new level of operation for the gangs in Haiti with his ascension to power.

They became more even empowered and terrorized the country day and night. Another gang known as Five Second (5 Segond) took the justice system by surprise; they invaded the courthouse. In June 2022, this social-media-savvy gang took over Haiti's largest courthouses with a type of weapon that looks like that of the military. They made use of drones and guns and attacked the whole court. They further weaken the court and judicial system by burning all the documents that have confidential files. They even seized computers that had pieces of evidence and cases pressuring the country. This gang did not stop attacking the judiciary alone but still went to attack a nearby National Port Authority and killed one person while getting two people injured.

Haiti is trying to survive between an unstable economy, a politically unstable country, and natural disasters that affect the country daily. Three months after the President's assassination, an earthquake claimed about 30 people's lives and rendered many buildings to their barest form in southwest Haiti.

Haiti had never been in its best state even before Jovenel came into power but reached its worst during his presidency. The country is currently suffering from the aftermath of the assassination and many political decisions made by past presidents. Haiti will continue to bear the brunt of the assassination now and in the coming years, and this will surface in many economic crises, insecurity, and corruption. But possibly, democracy can help restore all lost hope in Haiti.

{Outro}

It will take longer for Haiti to recover from this assassination, but the coin can toss either way. Haitians have been known to be survivors; it might take longer, but the country will wriggle its way out of its present predicament.

Do stay updated on all the episodes from this podcast by subscribing. I am looking forward to reading your comments and opinions.

Killing Jovenel

Episode 11: Restoring Constitutional Normalcy

{Intro}

Hello, welcome back to another episode of Azazel Podcast. In today's episode, I will give insights into what has been done so far to restore constitutional order in Haiti. When will the country hold an election, and when will a new president emerge? I will answer all those questions in this episode.

In the last episodes, I dropped insights into what has been happening in Haiti's political space after the assassination. How much havoc the gangs are causing in the country and the lives of citizens. With the increase in insecurity, gang rape is nothing to write about. But worry less; this episode will be much more intriguing as I will talk more about the journey to restoring constitutional order in Haiti.

{Segue}

Haiti is one country that has always had problems with its political state. During the presidency of Jovenel Moise, the status quo got worse as the country witnessed further political and social unrest. Jovenel Moise became president after he emerged as the winner in the 2016 election and was sworn in as president in February 2017. After he was sworn in, he started to gain political enemies. The more he sought to assert and expand his presidential power; the more his enemies grew in numbers. The president started ruling by decree in January 2020 after dismantling both the Supreme Court and Haiti electoral commission.

Killing Jovenel

After the massive protest against the Jovenel administration in 2019, he dismissed the Parliament and canceled the scheduled election for October 2019. To make matters worse, the opposition claimed that Jovenel extended his term by a year as he was denied holding power until 2021. His presidency only left a vacuum in the already broken system; there was no operative constitution and no working judicial system. That is one more reason why it has been so hard to have a president succeed him.

Ever since the assassination of Jovenel in July 2021, it has been hard to restore the country's constitutional order. Jovenel had left a power vacuum that cannot be solved alone by a presidential succession or even an election. The question of who will lead and who has the constitutional power to do so has continued to surface. The country has always had leaders who ruled through corrupt circles while showing their dictatorial part. To avoid these repeated circles, the 1987 constitution adopted by Haiti banned anyone from running as a president for two consecutive terms.

Usually, restoring a constitutional order would not have been that hard if Jovenel had not dismissed the electoral committee and seven Supreme Court judges. The modus operandi has always been stated in the constitution. Still, the absence of a viable President, legislature, legitimate prime minister, the judiciary, and the electoral commission has rendered the need to have a new president unattainable.

To restore constitutional order, Haitians in the country and diaspora have filed a consensus agreement with the political alliance known as PEN. This political alliance is to establish a presidential council with six seats for five members and prime ministers who will govern the country and lead a two-year transition as guided by the 1987 constitution.

The need for restoration led to the emergence of civil society platforms to lend a political voice to Haitians at home and abroad. That brought about the Montana and Louisiana accords, which have become more popular among Haitians. The Montana Accord emanated from the political alliance formed by Haitians in the country and Diaspora - PEN (Protocole d'Entente Nationale)

The Montana Accord, through its alliance, seems to come with full force and a show of political potency as they have started all plans towards having a two-year transitional government. The accord went ahead to select a President - Fritz Jean, a politically engaged economist and former head of the central bank, and a prime minister Steven Benoît, a former Haitian parliamentarian who had earlier participated In the Haiti 2015-16 general election, which was canceled. To show how much commitment they had, the alliance went ahead to. have a dialogue with Ariel Henry, Haiti's current Prime minister. Henry seems to both withdraw his support and, at the same time, show some level of interest.

But still, the international community is holding back even though Washington has withdrawn the endorsement for the Montana Accord.

Nonetheless, Haitians are not only stopping at the Montana Accord but went ahead with a Louisiana Accord/Summit. The idea for the summit was to ensure that Haitians in the diaspora can unify all the accords in Haiti and provide a framework that can guide whichever transitional government emerges in Haiti, but then the summit went sideways; it wasn't as expected. The accords present at the summit to unify all the agreements were Accord Montana, Accord Cesco, Accord Pen, Akor Lari'a, Accord Du Millieu, Accord Kontra Ped La, Accord Tribune Politiques Des Femmes. The summit organizers failed because instead of unifying the accords as stated, they chose to, under the control of the U.S. Army Retired General Honore, form a government where they elect a President and a Prime Minister.

The accords had a common goal of a better Haiti and a transitional government; at the summit, the accords both agreed to stick to having a president and a prime minister, and both decided to suggest names. Contrary to the opinion Montana had of Louisiana, the Louisiana accords wanted to lead Haiti for a very long term and did not buy the idea of a transitional government.

Montana and Louisiana accords have organized elections to elect presidents and a PM. Both accords elect the same presidents but different prime ministers. The September 11 accords supported Ariel, but that was different from the Louisiana accord that appointed a female interim prime minister, Mariam Fétièrre. Prime Minister Henry, in favor of a one-headed Government, remained firm on his positions but left an opening by evoking a possible ministerial reshuffle after February 7, 2022, to ease the crisis.

Haitians believed establishing this kind of alliance would restore a sense of peace in the country. In contrast, the need to restore democracy has been worked on since they had planned to build a pseudo-parliament to ensure checks and balances for the government they are about to create. It will also help wriggle them from the decisions of the international community on whom they elected as their president. Haitians were on a journey to free themselves from political meddling.

There have been about a thousand signatories to this accord. These signatories are leaders of organizations that served as representatives to millions of Haitians in the local and international space.

All these aside, Henry has planned to hold an election to restore constitutional order. However, still, it is hard to believe since there is no existing electoral committee or even a working Supreme Court to oversee the electoral activities. Henry is trying to restore election and constitutional order by bringing political parties and civil societies together to establish a functioning Provisional Electoral Council {PEC}.

Haiti's interim leader, Ariel Henry, is walking on a thin line, mainly because he has continued to show a non-commitment attitude to the reinstatement of constitutional order. Henry has only remained in power and existed as an interim leader only because he has always had the support of the international community. He has continued disregarding the constitutional order as he had planned to introduce a new constitution for the country. The country seems to run more or less like a lawless and anarchical country. This move of his is dangerous as it will only cost more lives of Haiti citizens.

In between a presidential succession and the restoration of constitutional order, the norm remains that Ariel Henry will continue to lead the Haitian government until another election, where a new president will appoint a new prime minister, which will be approved or rejected by a newly installed parliament.

{Outro}

The long walk of Haiti to constitutional freedom might take a long while and, at the same time, might happen soon; it is unpredictable. The country needs transformative leadership to enable its recovery from the losses the country has faced over many decades. Many have been claiming that Haiti needs a transitional government. At this crucial time, elections, harmony, community engagement, and political participation are necessary to deliver an ideal framework to create a lasting solution facing the country. The government must free itself from political intervention and meddling from the international community. It is time for Haiti to restore its constitutional order by herself.

I look forward to reading your thoughts on how the presidency can work for good in Haiti.

Enjoy the rest of the week!

Episode 12: Reigning

{Intro}

Hello, welcome back to another episode of Azazel Podcast. I will explain how Jovenel Moise ran his administration in today's episode. What was his presidency like? How did a businessman run the political stage of Haiti?

In the previous episodes, I gave snippets of how his administration had run, either by addressing him as an autocratic leader or showing how much he ruled by decree. However, in this episode, you will get access to premium information about how the administration had run before his death on July 07, 2021.

{Segue}

Jovenel Moise, known as Banana Man, took to Haiti's political stage after years in the Agribusiness, where he had a successful plantation farm and a Mechanic business - JOMAR Auto Parts. After his investment in Agribusiness, he started showing interest in politics, which he did by joining political organizations for the benefit of Agribusiness. He rose from membership to executive roles in this organization and showed interest in being President in 2015. His interest was further furnished after the previous President - Mr. Martelly, appointed him as his preferred presidential candidate. The 2015 election was annulled, and he was elected President in November 2016 by winning 55% of the total votes.

He was sworn in as Haiti's 58th President in February 2017. His inauguration as the President brought an end to an extended and complicated two-year election cycle. His swearing-in came with the hope for change since the country has just witnessed a political crisis that lasted more than a year and even natural disasters that have further thrown the country into one of the countries with a high poverty rate.

As President, Jovenel inherited a country with a struggling economy and a divided society. To make the matter worse, his administration started with an unresolved judicial investigation on loans for his agribusiness. It was believed that a confidential report on laundered money had leaked during his campaign, even though the President dismissed the claim and only attributed it to the opposition party's doings.

Jovenel also stated in an interview that he would ensure that the Justice system would not be a ground for public persecution in his administration. Whether or not? We will know.

During his administration, Jovenel tried to ensure that there were power dynamics and that the power was not only concentrated in the hands of Haiti's rich and powerful people. For instance, the electricity contracts have always been given to oligarchs of Haiti, but instead of providing light, they made the country dwell more in darkness.

Unknown to Jovenel, the more he fought the oligarchs, the more he became one himself. He was so engrossed in fighting the opposition party that he forgot that only a warrior who runs from the waterfront would see to fighting another war. Even though Jovenel was trying to set the system straight by ending the monopoly, the system only became a means to end his life and the beginning of a journey to his assassination.

Amidst all these is the President's most remarkable flagship policy - Caravan for Change. The policy, which started in the first year of his administration, was to implement and address the need for new infrastructures and other necessities for development in Haiti. These structures have been lacking for quite a while in the country.

Interestingly, the Caravan for Change did have some impressive achievements. There has been remarkable excellence in different areas that ranged from health care to energy to education and even to environment and infrastructures. Over 200 kilometers of the road were built and renovated in a year of his administration. The policy also cleaned eleven rivers and rehabilitated eight hospitals and health centers. In the area of education, 400 classrooms were renovated.

Unfortunately, his death was a stumbling block to many changes he believed he would get done before he handed over power. Among these was the electricity strategy. The President had earlier stated in an interview with Forbes how he would execute the electricity strategy.

The strategy embodied three significant components: building and reconstructing the old national grid, building microgrids to enable decentralized and independent power sources, and provisioning electricity for scarcely populated areas through standalone power systems. These were big projects and would take a lot of commitment and dedication for their execution.

Not only had Jovenel imagined Haiti having a significant leap in infrastructure development through his administration, but he envisioned the country becoming a renewable energy powerhouse. In fulfilling some of these dreams, the Haiti Parliament September 2017 abolished import tariffs and duties on solar equipment to encourage as much growth in the renewable energy industry as possible. The vision of the Jovenel administration for Haiti was to leapfrog the fossil fuel industry and construct traditional grids to achieve an energy-independent country with a high level of economic stability.

A few years into his administration, his call for resignation mounted from different parts of the country. The only way to save himself from unfavorable impeachment was to start ruling by decree. But then, Jovenel Moïse supporters described his administration as that which was to take the fall of a country deeply rooted in corruption.

{Outro}

The Jovenel administration came with the hope for change and a new system to make history. While it prophesies a significant difference, it was partly written of violence, gangraping, and many despicable activities. To end it all, the administration ended with the President's assassination. Sad, isn't it?

A banana man whose administration all hoped for a better country rested couldn't fulfill the promise to many citizens of

Haiti, especially with his death that still plunges the country day and night.

All hope is not lost, but that is only if democracy is restored in Haiti.

Don't forget to subscribe to the podcast and stay tuned for more from the podcast.

Episode 13: Legacy

{Intro}

Hello, welcome back to another episode of Azazel Podcast. In today's episode, which is the last episode, I will be talking about Jovenel Moise. Today, I will discuss whether his clamor to run for the Presidency was all a lie. Maybe he didn't have the intention after all and had only become president because the president before him had appointed him. Or, better still, he wanted to revive Haiti's economic and political instability.

To recap, in the previous episodes, I gave an explanation and an analysis of who Jovenel was, how he attained the political stage, how his administration was, what changed in his administration as to the way Haiti has always been run, the state of democracy in Haiti and now how the whole running for election came by for him.

{Segue}

The will to be and be voted for is the mantra of democracy. That should have been the note on which Jovenel should have lived his life as a president. He came to power after the previous President, Martelly, appointed him; he came in as the president after he won the second election. He became president, and not quite long after his ascension; he started acting contrary to his promise to the Haiti populace.

These happenings have indeed called for whether Jovenel had wanted to be a president or maybe he only contested because it would be a much better avenue to finance his businesses.

The suspicion was further fuelled by the people of Haiti calling for his resignation after the country saw the president's supposed involvement in looting about $2 billion from the government's Petrocaribe Fund. How accurate was this claim, and how much can we say this was his true intention?

That claim was found to be true in the report that was released in May 2019. The information compiled by Haiti's Superior Court of Auditors and Administrative Disputes (CSCCA) had Moïse's companies accused of bilking the Venezuelan oil-fed Petrocaribe Fund of about $2 million. It is becoming more accurate; no wonder by 2020, the president had already started to rule by decree to show that he was covering his steps outrightly. He began leading by decree months after his administration failed to hold scheduled legislative elections in October 2019.

Many critics blamed him for postponing the earlier scheduled parliament elections meant to be held in October 2019 and finally leaving the country without a parliament. His opponent even further questioned why he had to rule by decree and was elected as a democratic leader, but he is doing just otherwise.

In his defense, Jovenel told the opponents and his critics that he is committed to democracy and would use the remaining year of his administration to ensure that local, municipal legislative, and presidential elections are held in October 2021. Unknown to him that he will die before the election takes place.

Killing Jovenel

The president tried to overpower anyone who deemed his administration illegitimate, and he issued a decree to send the top members of the Supreme Court, including Judges Dabresil and Jean-Louis, into retirement. Ironically, this is the height of what a president should stand for.

In a bid to overshadow the existence of his being in the Presidency, he claimed to be planning a referendum to overhaul Haiti's constitution, which he argues needs to be modernized. But then, Jovenel's opponents and critics still think that's all a lie, and his intention was far from pure. That fear was that his purpose for the referendum was to get rid of the clause which bans presidents from serving two consecutive terms in office so that he can run again for Presidency in September. His assassination all cut his plans short.

Power begets power; that is the final phrase I can put on what most have made Jovenel look like his clamor for Presidency is a lie. To some, he was a monster who stole their daily bread and sense of belonging but to others; he was a messiah who sought to take Haiti from years of economic imbalance, political instability, and natural disasters.

As he tried his best as a president, he became the scapegoat of the opposition, looking to sacrifice him for a long while, even before the Columbians assassinated him. To think the people who wanted him to resign didn't know his assassination will do the country no good. Still, it will make the country susceptible to violence, daylight kidnapping and shooting, and other acts of violence that have put the country in a tight place to make the best decision for themselves.

Haiti has come a long way and will continue to make the long walk to freedom. But the walk can either be through a transitional government or the parliament who are in thirst for power.

Whichever country chooses to adopt will either be a risk or a win. At the same time, it can be a risk-win for the country

{Outro}

Thank you for staying till the end of this episode on Jovenel Moise, the discussion on his assassination, and the state of Haiti's political stage after his demise. The story of how a banana man got to become a president and how towards his administration, he was assassinated would not have been complete without the listeners. Do stay tuned for more juicy and exciting content.

I look forward to reading your thoughts on what the future holds for Haiti, will there ever be normalcy?

Enjoy the rest of the week, and do not forget to subscribe to Azazel Podcast!

Episode 14: Surviving Democracy

{Intro}

Hello, welcome back to another episode of Azazel Podcast. In today's episode, I will give insights into what has been done so far to restore constitutional order in Haiti. When will the election be, and when will a new president emerge? I will answer all those questions in this episode.

In the last episode, I spoke on what has been done so far to restore constitutional order in Haiti, how an election can only be a means to survival in Haiti but cannot put an end to its current predicament

{Segue}

The term survival of the fittest has never applied to many as it did to Haiti and the state of its democracy. The democratic institution, which is on the brink of failure, has to find its way to survive since it seems that is where the hope of a peaceful country for the citizens of Haiti rests.

Since the ascension of President Jovenel Moïse, the democracy in Haiti has become something to be forgotten. The president ruled by decree for almost two years, extended his tenure by a year, and dismissed anything about the election. All his actions only break the institution called democracy the more. Then came the president's assassination, which was clear proof that the democratic system in Haiti was completely broken.

In the wake of his assassination, Haiti had no democratic institution, which made the tussle for power a difficult one to come by. In a situation where Haiti's democracy was working, an election would have been conducted, or better still, there would have been a change in power to someone who had the development of the country at hand.

But the question remains how will democracy survive? Can it survive amid gang violence, insecurities, terrorism, kidnapping, foreign interferences, and political meddling?

The view is that matter who Haitians vote for during elections, the international community would still pick the winners they wanted, as was the case during the election in 2011 that had the International community choose President Martelly, who had come third in the election. Political meddling is one of the reasons democracy might not survive another day, as it only increases the sentiments that elections do not necessarily equate to participatory democracy.

By the look of things, it can survive, as many Haiti citizens have been in search of a lasting solution to the country's political crisis. There has been a coalition between the civil society groups in Haiti to form an accord known as the Montana Accord. The alliance is to present a two-year transformational government that will bring back democratic institutions and re-establish the lost trust and legitimacy of the Haiti government.

This is the best shot to keep Haiti's Democracy alive since it will only take the absence of gangs and the reduction of violence in Haiti before the masses can be outside to exercise their franchise. It is noteworthy that Haiti's democracy is now at a critical point - one that has faced degradation and had no hope of surviving or returning to normalcy. It is even more tempting to think a new election is a way for democracy to stay in Haiti and the final lap to restoring stability in the country.

But with the country's experience of bad leaders, it is known that the survival of Haiti's democracy lies in the opposite direction; the government needs to fix the broken system. Haitian democracy has been declining for years, and with the rise in insecurities in Haiti, the decline has accelerated. Each election only increases the loopholes in the system, further rendering the institution weak.

The democratic governance is sliding backward, and to survive this harsh reality facing the Haiti democracy, Haitians must look for ways to establish new rules in the game and play by it so well. They must work on who determines the rule the game plays by since elections rely on a relationship between the states and the citizens, and it is an agreement where the citizens agree to the state's rules which governs how they choose their leaders. Although electing a leader is always spelled out in the constitution, with the absence of a working democratic institution in Haiti, the country must have new rules, and the game needs to change.

Until Haiti is safe enough to accommodate its citizens in a peaceful environment, will democracy come back to reality? But to make the institution survive, it is only enough for people to vote freely when the state of security and democratic institutions are strengthened. By that, Haiti would only be going through the indications of a democratic state rather than putting in place a government elected by the people.

This process of who will decide when and how the election will take place will determine whether Haiti's democracy will survive and whether the next election will enjoy legitimacy and the rightful mandate.

For democracy to survive in Haiti, the relevant agency must amend the Haiti 1987 constitution. The constitution has left many gaps, including the power division between the Presidents and the parliament. There needs to be the provision of a permanent electoral council and the need for a new electoral law since each election means that the parliament in every electoral cycle renegotiates the process.

{Outro}

A country by the people for the people will take decades or even scores before it can become a reality in present-day Haiti. The country is on the brink of falling, and even the democracy might not be able to survive except with transformative leadership and elections, as opined in the last episode.

I look forward to reading your comments on Haiti's democracy and how you think it can survive amidst the struggles and chaos in the country.

Enjoy the rest of the week!

Episode 15: The Day After

{Intro}

Hello, welcome back to another episode of Azazel Podcast. In today's episode, I will give insights on whether there is a possibility of democracy in Haiti ever again. With the look of things in Haiti, is there hope for democracy? If at all democracy did survive, as explained in the last episode, would it be the same democracy as it has always been known? Possibly Yes.

In the last episode, I mentioned how far democracy in Haiti can survive, how long it will take, and what restructuring needs to be done to make the country's democracy survive.

Let us do a reality check together, Shall we?

{Segue}

Haiti has always had a history of democracy, from throwing off the French Colonial rule to gaining independence and selecting its leaders. This need for its government made Haiti the first independent state in Latin America and the Caribbean in the early 19th century and the first Black-led Republic. This history only emphasizes how far Haiti has come in terms of democracy.

Democracy has become a thin line of hope for the people in Haiti, especially after the president's assassination. Jovenel Moise, the country's president, was elected to power in 2016, and a few years after his ascension into power, he started ruling by decree. He continued to stall the progress of conducting a parliamentary election in Haiti. From there, the dismissal of the parliament began, and then the judiciary. That killed the next of kin into the power of the presidency, according to the 1987 constitution of Haiti.

This selfish act of Jovenel only jeopardizes the future of the country's democracy, a democracy that was never stable before. Even after his death, there is no sign of recovery in sight for Haiti's Democracy; there is no electoral committee to conduct a free and fair election, no existing parliament, and not even the presence of the Supreme Court Judges. Saddening, isn't it?

His assassination further raises a level of uncertainty among the citizens of Haiti about the country's democracy. Haiti has always had a history of political meddling from international communities, which has affected its democracy. Foreign interference has taken its toll on Haiti's democracy, and even many citizens have lost their trust and credibility in the system.

The mode of operation in Haiti's democratic system is called bicephalic. In a bicephalic system, an elected president appoints a prime minister from an existing parliament in the country. This system swore in Ariel Henry, the prime minister that was appointed by Jovenel just a day before his assassination.

Just like Jovenel, Henry has never been the people's man and was even accused of being an unconstitutional prime minister. In defense, Henry only acclaimed that he was still pushing for a democratic institution. Still, then, there is a need to put elections on hold in Haiti because of the country's state of insecurity.

Does this mean that democracy will take a long while to be possible in Haiti?

The daily insecurity level in Haiti has rendered many destitute and has increased migration to other countries in the last few years. And so, it is much better to stay safe and wait till the country becomes safe for an election to happen or, better still, have an election and have the credibility questioned.

Outrightly, one could reasonably say that the postponement of elections in Haiti is to increase the functionality of Haiti's democracy as a free and fair one. It is to increase the possibility of democracy in Haiti ever again. But while the reasons might be valid, Haiti has never been known as a peaceful country. Does that mean the government will never hold an election in future years? Or can we say Henry is a messiah for Haiti in this time of need? Does his postponement of elections have anything to do with him increasing the possibility that an election might take place in Haiti?

In the past years, the idea of democracy ever resurfacing in Haiti was dead as Haiti was under the dynastic Duvalier dictatorship for twenty-nine years. But then, democracy came back into existence, and just again, Jovenel shattered that hope by ruling with a decree. This only shows that history can still repeat itself, and the possibility of democracy in Haiti will come again.

February 7 remains a remarkable date in the history of democracy revival in Haiti. It explains more than the surface of it is a date for the inauguration of a new president. The day only reminds Haiti of the significance of their struggles for democracy, that which had caused more lives of Haitians for many decades.

{Outro}

All hope is not lost, and the idea of democracy ever again in Haiti is something to which every citizen of Haiti looks forward. This is why there have been both the Montana and Louisiana accords to ensure a transitional government that can further provide a democratic institution. And yes, there is still a possibility of democracy in Haiti ever again, and this will happen if Henry holds on to his promise and organizes a free and fair election.

Thank you for listening to the podcast, don't forget to hit the subscribe and alarm button.

See you all!!

Episode 16: Dying Before his Birth

{Intro}

Hello, welcome back to another episode of Azazel Podcast. I am taking a different turn from our previous episodes in today's episode. I'll be talking about the deaths Jovenel encountered even before the Colombians actually killed him. He has always been a living corpse, and his actual killing only brought to the limelight many deaths he was facing.

In a previous episode, I mentioned how much is needed to be in place for democracy to be back to normalcy in Haiti and emphasized that hope is never lost for the people of Haiti to witness peace again.

You do want to listen to how much information I hold with me, don't you?

{Segue}

Every man shall die once is a statement that can be inferred not true. While man is buried only once, our death can occur many times, even in our lifetime. And this is the tale of Jovenel Moïse. A man who was indeed oblivious to his many encounters with death.

Why? Because he has been faced with numerous challenges unknown to him, he died years back, even before his assassination. The more he gets closer to fueling his political ambition; the more his death draws nearer. From the day he started the step of leaving for Port-au-Prince and becoming a banana man, to becoming a Social Entrepreneur and eventually contesting for his first election in 2015. Unknown to him, the moment he assumed Haiti's leadership mantle was when he started to be at loggerheads with Haiti's oligarchs that wanted puppets as president. Jovenel was trying to remove power from some powerful groups in Haiti that owned over 90% of the country's resources.

Jovenel Moise, born in 1968, started his political career by joining the Agribusiness associations and later contesting for the presidency in 2015, but that election was annulled. While Jovenel might think it was a bad thing back then, I feel it was God's warning for him to let him know that if he ever won the election, his final burial would be closer than he thought. But fortunately, or unfortunately for him, he emerged as the president in 2017, and his woes began. After years of fighting the richest, he almost became one himself, and in the process, he was savagely assassinated.

To those who seem to think that only Jovenel was murdered that day or that Jovenel was murdered on that day, let me reiterate that it was Haiti that murdered that day, and Jovenel was assassinated before he was even born. He was not the only president who knew such a fate. To the likes, I cite Jean-Jacques Dessalines, Toussaint Louverture, Dumarsais Estime, Jean-Bertrand Aristide, and Jovenel Moïse. Because their economic policies would have reduced the poverty gap and provided economic opportunities for the people to pursue the

Haitian Dream, they infuriated Haiti's elite and their international backers. As a result, the country suffers as they are labeled as dictators, out of touch, gang enablers, and other similar degrading terms. Note that Aristide was impeached in 2004 and overthrown twice by the Haitian Military because he fought against the oligarchs back then, the same applied to Dumarsais Estimé, who the U.S. Army overthrew in 1950.

But one thing is evident, with Jovenel's story, history was fast repeating itself in Haiti. From Haiti's first democratic leader - Jean-Bertrand Aristide, to Jovenel, who might be the last democratic leader of Haiti, the status quo has been the same with these two men. They have always been a victim of those who are not patriotic to Haiti.

Throughout the history of Haiti, the U.S. has been actively engaged in undermining the legitimacy of Haitian leaders who refused to bow to American imperialism. Back in the 1940s, the U.S. had trained an army who were specifically tasked with overthrowing Haiti leaders that were popular with the locals but rejected by the U.S., and Dumarsais was the first to be a victim. Haiti enjoyed political and social stability under his administration, but after the Core Group overthrew him, the political trajectory changed. And then, by 1991, Jean-Bertrand Aristide, a poor Roman-Catholic priest, came into power through his anti-imperialism view. Still, he was soon a victim himself when he attempted to hold accountable influential business leaders with strong ties to Washington. His administration had back and forth as he had to go through the process of restoration and elimination from power. He can be said to be the strongest to withstand power struggles in the history of Haiti.

Aristide resigned from pressures exerted by the U.S. and armed rebellions in Haiti. Aristide's forced resignation came only nine years after the U.S. military helped him regain power after a military coup. Aristide resigned intending to curtail violence in Haiti, which he did with the remark in his resignation letter, Life for everyone, death for no one but unknown to him, Haiti will grow in violence and gang killing in the few years to come.

This must have also been what Jovenel imagined when he was faced with a gruesome death, but behind his assassination is the lives of many Haitians who have witnessed deaths and many whose deaths have passed. His killing only gave more power to the oligarchs and even the U.S., who knew Jovenel would be an obstacle to their foreign policy agenda in Haiti.

Because of his death, The Security Council of the U.N. is considering creating a sanctions regime that may lead to a military or armed forces occupation of Haiti like they did after they removed Aristide in 2004. In 2004, U.N. peacekeepers were deployed to Haiti after a rebellion that led to the exile of then-President Jean-Bertrand Aristide. These peacekeeping troops left only after 13 years and were replaced by the U.N. police, who left in 2019.

This situation may even apply to Haiti now, especially with Jovenel's demise and the rise in political instability in the country. The U.S. government may decide to send another peacekeeping force, particularly with the clamor for U.N. support by the people of Haiti. The U.S. may do so under the pretext of working with the government to strengthen political stability and good governance, rights protection, and justice reform and help organize free and fair elections. But obviously, this is only a facade to cover their true intentions: to hold Haiti under their grip. They want Haiti to keep running back to them whenever there is political instability, and the more that happens, the more the need to hold Haiti tighter.

However, what will forever be known in history is that Haiti died the moment Jovenel was killed, Haiti has been dying when Aristide was impeached in 2004, and this will forever continue to occur if the Haiti oligarchs exist and if the U.S. and other International Community continue to meddle in Haiti affairs.

Printed in Great Britain
by Amazon